Josh Hamilton and Debra Monk in a scene from the New York production of "Women and Wallace." Set design by Allen Moyer.

WOMEN AND WALLACE

BY JONATHAN MARC SHERMAN

★

★

DRAMATISTS
PLAY SERVICE
INC.

For Maria, who justifies romance.

WOMEN AND WALLACE was first produced at Playwrights Horizons in the fall of 1988 as part of the Foundation of the Dramatists Guild's Seventh Annual Playwrights Festival, (Producing Director, Nancy Quinn.) It was directed by Don Scardino, with sets by Allen Moyer, costumes by Jess Goldstein, and lighting by Nancy Schertler. The production stage manager was Roy Harris and the playwright advisor was Albert Innaurato. Music was composed and performed by John Miller. The cast, in order of appearance, was as follows:

WALLACE KIRKMAN.	Josh Hamilton
NINA	Joanna Going
MOTHER	Mary Joy
GRANDMOTHER	Joan Copeland
VICTORIA	Dana Behr
PSYCHIATRIST	Debra Monk
SARAH	Bellina Logan
LILI	Jill Tasker
WENDY	Erica Gimpel

Characters

Wallace Kirkman.
Nina.
Mother.
Grandmother.
Victoria.
Psychiatrist.
Sarah.
Lili.
Wendy.

Time

1975 to 1987.

Note

All sets and props should be simple and spare. The lighting should be very suggestive. Scenes should flow quickly from one to the next. The actor playing Wallace should be about

4

eighteen years old. The women's parts can be played in one of three ways.

1. One virtuoso actress can play them all, which is the idea I had in mind when I started but which scares the hell out of me now.
2. Three or four actresses can be used, each one playing more than one part. I would be careful about giving the actresses playing both Nina and Mother more than one part, for various reasons.
3. Eight actresses can be used, with one part per actress. This is, I think, the most desirable solution, but may be tough to achieve.

The four times that Wallace reads his writing directly to the audience can be handled simply by having him speak right to the audience, without a piece of paper before him or anything. The title is, so far, the only title I can stand, as well as being the first thing I called the play. **Be Wonderful.**

Order of Scenes

"The great question that has never been answered, and which I have not been able to answer, despite my thirty years of research into the feminine soul, is: What does a woman want?" — Sigmund Freud.

WOMEN AND WALLACE

Wallace is standing to the left with a tomato in his hand and a crate of tomatoes at his feet. Nina is standing to the right, wearing a white dress. Pause. Wallace lobs the tomato. It splatters on Nina's dress. Pause.

WALLACE. I love you. (*Pause.*)

SCENE ONE

Wallace.

WALLACE. "Mommy". By Wallace Kirkman. Age six. I love Mommy because she makes me peanut butter and banana sandwiches on Wonder bread and it tastes better than when I order it at a restaurant. And Mommy never looks at me funny like the waiters in restaurants do. And Mommy crushes aspirins and mixes them into jelly when I get sick. Because I can't swallow aspirins. They just sit on my tongue and wait for me to finish the whole glass of water. And then I spit them out. But when they're mixed into jelly, I hardly have any problem at all. I just eat the jelly and feel better. And Mommy washes my clothes, so I don't have to. And she does it so they all smell nice when they come out. They come out smelling clean. And they even smell a little like Mommy, because she folds them for me, and her smell rubs off onto my shirts. She smells like perfume. Not really sweet, like Billy Corkscraw's mother. Mommy smells like she's getting ready to go out to dinner. And Mommy's read every book in the library downstairs. I couldn't do that. She can read three books in a week with no trouble at all. Real books, not The Hardy Boys. Mommy's really smart. She can read and take care of me. Both. That's why I love Mommy.

7

Scene Two

The kitchen. Mother is fixing a peanut butter and banana sandwich with a large knife. She puts it into a lunchbox on the table. Wallace runs in.

WALLACE. I'm going to miss the bus! Is my lunch ready?
MOTHER. All set. (*Wallace grabs the lunchbox and kisses Mother on the cheek.*)
WALLACE. Bye, Mommy.
MOTHER. Bye, Wallace.
WALLACE. (*To the audience.*) I love the second grade!
MOTHER. Don't shout, Wallace. (*Wallace runs out. Mother watches after him. She writes a note on a slip of paper and puts it on the table. She takes off her turtleneck shirt, so she is in her brassiere. She slits her throat with the large knife. She falls to the floor. Pause. Wallace runs in.*)
WALLACE. Mommy, I'm home! (*Wallace sees Mother on the floor. He picks up the note. Reading the note.*) "Cremate the parasite."

Scene Three

Wallace's bedroom. Wallace is laying on his bed. Grandmother walks in, holding a gift and a photograph.

GRANDMOTHER. Here you are. Your teacher gave me this gift for you.
WALLACE. It's not my birthday.
GRANDMOTHER. Well, something bad happened to you. When something bad happens, you get gifts to make you feel better.
WALLACE. Why do I get gifts on my birthday?
GRANDMOTHER. Well, because you're a year older.
WALLACE. Being a year older isn't bad.
GRANDMOTHER. It adds up. Open your gift. (*Wallace opens his gift.*)
WALLACE. Peanut brittle.
GRANDMOTHER. Isn't that *lovely*—
WALLACE. I *hate* peanut brittle.

8

GRANDMOTHER. So do I. Don't forget to send your teacher a thank you note.

WALLACE. Why should I *send* her something? I see her every day.

GRANDMOTHER. So *give* her a thank you note.

WALLACE. But I *hate* peanut brittle.

GRANDMOTHER. So throw the peanut brittle at her during the pledge of allegiance. Just give her *something* in return for her gift. It's good manners.

WALLACE. Okay.

GRANDMOTHER. She's a very pretty woman.

WALLACE. I guess so.

GRANDMOTHER. Why aren't you downstairs?

WALLACE. Too many people. Why'd they all come back home with us?

GRANDMOTHER. I don't know. They didn't get enough grief out, maybe.

WALLACE. I think they just like free food.

GRANDMOTHER. You're probably right. They're all bunched together like a big black cloud of perfume and cologne munching on little corned beef sandwiches. *Horrible.*

WALLACE. What's that?

GRANDMOTHER. What? *This?*

WALLACE. Yeah.

GRANDMOTHER. Oh, it's a photograph of your mother. The last one, as far as I know. Your father took it six days ago. I wanted to have it.

WALLACE. I wish Mommy would come back.

GRANDMOTHER. I know, Wallace, but for whatever reasons, she wanted to go —

WALLACE. She didn't want to.

GRANDMOTHER. What? Wallace —

WALLACE. I know she didn't want to, Grandma, I know. A pirate came in while I was at school and tore her open. He took everything inside of her and put it in his sack and escaped through the kitchen door. She didn't want to go, Grandma. And if I was here — if I pretended I was sick and stayed home — I could have saved her —

GRANDMOTHER. No. You couldn't have. Don't think

9

you could have saved her, because I'm telling you, you couldn't have. Nobody could have. It was time for her to go. It'll be time for me to go soon, too. And someday, it'll be your time to go—

WALLACE. Not me. I'm going to live forever.

GRANDMOTHER. I wish you luck. You'd be the first person to do it.

WALLACE. I'm going to.

GRANDMOTHER. If anybody can, Wallace, I'm sure it'll be you.

WALLACE. And I'm going to find the pirate who did this. You wait and see.

GRANDMOTHER. I will, Wallace. I certainly will. (*Pause.*) You look very handsome in your suit.

WALLACE. Thank you.

Scene Four

The schoolyard. Wallace is sitting on a bench, eating a sandwich. Victoria walks in.

VICTORIA. Hi, Wallace.

WALLACE. Hi, Victoria.

VICTORIA. Can I sit down?

WALLACE. Free country. (*Victoria sits down next to Wallace.*)

VICTORIA. What you got for lunch?

WALLACE. Peanut butter and banana.

VICTORIA. Want to trade?

WALLACE. What do you have?

VICTORIA. Tuna.

WALLACE. No, thanks. Besides, I already ate some of mine.

VICTORIA. Peanut butter and banana's my favorite. Bet it's good.

WALLACE. It kind of sucks. My Dad made it. Dads can't make lunch. You can barely *taste* the banana.

VICTORIA. (*Pause.*) I'm sorry about your mother.

WALLACE. Yeah. Me, too.

VICTORIA. She killed herself?

WALLACE. Who told you that?

10

VICTORIA. I don't know. Somebody.
WALLACE. She didn't kill herself. A pirate slit her throat, I think. I haven't finished checking things out yet.
VICTORIA. Uh uh. That's not what they said. They said "suicide".
WALLACE. Who cares?
VICTORIA. I don't know. (*Pause.*) You want a hug?
WALLACE. (*Quiet.*) Yeah. (*Victoria hugs Wallace for a few moments. He pushes her away suddenly and she falls.*) Get away from me! (*Pause.*) I gotta go. (*Wallace runs out. Pause. Victoria walks over to Wallace's sandwich and looks at it. She picks it up and takes a bite.*)

SCENE FIVE

Wallace.

WALLACE. "Broken Glass." By Wallace Kirkman. Age thirteen. It's past four in the morning and I can't sleep. I go downstairs to get something to drink and maybe see what's on television. I open the refrigerator and take out the orange juice. I drink orange juice because I'm susceptible to colds. And because I heard that Coke rots your teeth. Whether it does or not makes no difference, because after you hear something like that, it stays in your brain. So I pour some orange juice into a glass and put the carton back in the fridge. And I drink. It goes down smooth and cold, and I just swallow it all without stopping. When I'm done, I look at the empty glass in my hand. My parents got a truckload of glassware for their wedding, and the glass in my hand is one of the set. It's older than me. Respect your elders, I think, but then I see her. She's laughing at me. She's inside the glass, laughing at me. I throw the glass against the refrigerator and hear it crash. I look at the shards on the floor. Like an invitation. I know that glass is made of sand, and I like walking on the beach, and I almost step towards the glass, but I don't. I think of blood. My blood. And I just kneel down and stare at the broken glass on the floor, watching for any reflection of the moonlight outside the kitchen window and waiting for my father to come downstairs, because he can't sleep through anything.

11

SCENE SIX

Psychiatrist's office. Psychiatrist is sitting in a chair, writing in a notebook. Wallace walks in.

PSYCHIATRIST. You must be *Wallace.*
WALLACE. Yeah, I'm him.
PSYCHIATRIST. Pleased to meet you. Would you like to have a seat?
WALLACE. Can I lie on the couch?
PSYCHIATRIST. If you'd like.
WALLACE. It seems like the proper thing to do.
PSYCHIATRIST. Go right ahead.
WALLACE. I should *warn* you that I've had my head measured by a close friend, and if you shrink it by so much as a *millimeter*, I'm taking you to *court.*
PSYCHIATRIST. I don't shrink heads.
WALLACE. If I say "*I* do", does that make me insane?
PSYCHIATRIST. It's not that simple. (*Wallace lies down on the couch.*)
WALLACE. Nice couch. Where'd you get it?
PSYCHIATRIST. Bloomingdale's.
WALLACE. Really? I would have thought there'd be some store that would sell special couches for psychiatrists. It doesn't feel as good when you know that anybody with a few bucks can get one.
PSYCHIATRIST. Tell me why you're here, Wallace.
WALLACE. It was either this or a straitjacket, I suppose.
PSYCHIATRIST. Why's that?
WALLACE. Come on, didn't my father tell you all this?
PSYCHIATRIST. I'd like to hear what you have to say.
WALLACE. Can't argue with that. You see, I've been breaking glasses. In the kitchen.
PSYCHIATRIST. Any particular reason?
WALLACE. I like to live dangerously. You know, in perpetual fear of slicing the soles of my feet open. I don't know what it is, but ever since they cut the umbilical cord, I've been obsessed with *sharp* things. Especially knives. I'm attracted to knives. I'm *incredibly* attracted to *doctors* with knives. Do *you* have a knife, doctor?

12

PSYCHIATRIST. No—

WALLACE. Do you want to *buy* one?

PSYCHIATRIST. No.

WALLACE. Oh. (*Long pause.*)

PSYCHIATRIST. Tell me about your mother, Wallace.

WALLACE. She was like Sylvia Plath without the publishing contract.

PSYCHIATRIST. Do you remember much about her?

WALLACE. *Nothing.*

PSYCHIATRIST. Nothing at all?

WALLACE. Nope.

PSYCHIATRIST. Are you sure?

WALLACE. Why are you asking me this? Tell me, would you ask me this if my father weren't paying you?

PSYCHIATRIST. You're upset because your father made you come here.

WALLACE. No, I'm upset because he didn't pick a prettier psychiatrist.

PSYCHIATRIST. Was your *mother* pretty, Wallace?

WALLACE. (*Pause.*) Yeah, she was pretty. *Pretty* pretty. Pretty *suicidal.* And now she's pretty *dead.*

PSYCHIATRIST. You know, Wallace, you don't have to say anything you don't *want* to say.

WALLACE. Okay. (*Long silence.*)

PSYCHIATRIST. What are you thinking about, Wallace? (*Pause.*) Wallace? (*Pause.*) Wallace?

SCENE SEVEN

The park. Wallace and Victoria walk in. Wallace is eating a Mallo Cup and drinking something pink out of a bottle. Victoria is eating Jujyfruits.

VICTORIA. Good movie.

WALLACE. Yeah.

VICTORIA. I like the kissing stuff.

WALLACE. I like when the girl died.

VICTORIA. You want to sit down here?

WALLACE. Here?

VICTORIA. Yeah. Sure.

13

WALLACE. Yeah. Sure. (*Wallace and Victoria sit down on a bench.*)

VICTORIA. You want a Jujyfruit?

WALLACE. No, they stick to your teeth. You want a Mallo Cup?

VICTORIA. Chocolate makes you break out.

WALLACE. Oh. (*Wallace takes a bite out of a Mallo Cup and drinks from his bottle.*)

VICTORIA. What is that?

WALLACE. What is *what?*

VICTORIA. *That.* In the bottle. The pink stuff.

WALLACE. Oh. You don't want to know.

VICTORIA. Sure I do. Wouldn't ask if I didn't want to know.

WALLACE. Uh, well, it's Pepto Bismol mixed with seltzer.

VICTORIA. *What?*

WALLACE. I've got this perpetually upset stomach, and drinking this helps. It isn't all that bad, actually. Want some?

VICTORIA. No, thanks. I'll pass. (*Pause.*) It's such a nice day.

WALLACE. Yeah, it's not bad.

VICTORIA. I don't want to go back to school. Do you?

WALLACE. Oh, I'm just *dying* to sharpen my pencils and do tons of homework every night.

VICTORIA. Do you think eighth grade is going to be any different than seventh grade?

WALLACE. No chance in hell. It's all the same. I don't think it matters. They just keep us in school until we're safely through our growth spurts and all of the puberty confusion, then send us out to make the best of the rest of our lives. And we get so terrified of the real world that we pay some university to keep us for four more years or eight more years or whatever. It all depends on how terrified you are. My grandmother's brother is sixty-two, he's *still* taking classes up in Chicago. If they keep you long enough to get comfortable when you're young, they've got you for *life.*

VICTORIA. Not me, that's for sure. Once I'm out, I'm *out.* I'm not going to college, no *way.*

WALLACE. What are you going to do?

VICTORIA. Who knows? Sit on the beach and get a really

solid tan. Watch a lot of movies. Dance.

WALLACE. Sounds pretty stimulating, Victoria.

VICTORIA. Don't tease me.

WALLACE. I wasn't.

VICTORIA. Yes, you were.

WALLACE. I swear, I was not teasing you. Why would I tease you?

VICTORIA. I don't know. (*Pause.*) You didn't like the kissing stuff?

WALLACE. Huh?

VICTORIA. You know, in the movie.

WALLACE. Oh, I don't know.

VICTORIA. Sure you do.

WALLACE. I was getting candy. I missed it. Leave me alone.

VICTORIA. You want to try?

WALLACE. Try what?

VICTORIA. *That.*

WALLACE. What's *that*?

VICTORIA. Kissing.

WALLACE. You mean, with *you*?

VICTORIA. Yeah.

WALLACE. You mean, *now*?

VICTORIA. Yeah.

WALLACE. Umm —

VICTORIA. Scared?

WALLACE. Yeah, *right*. Go ahead. Kiss me.

VICTORIA. You sure?

WALLACE. As Shore as Dinah.

VICTORIA. *Dinah*?

WALLACE. Forget it. Will you kiss me already?

VICTORIA. Okay. (*Victoria takes out the Jujyfruit she was eating and throws it away. They kiss.*)

WALLACE. You didn't fade out.

VICTORIA. Nope.

WALLACE. I think I love you, Victoria.

VICTORIA. Really? (*Wallace grabs Victoria and starts kissing her with great passion, holding her in his arms. After a few moments, she breaks away.*)

WALLACE. What's wrong?

15

VICTORIA. What's *wrong*? You're too *fast* for me, Wallace, *that's* what's wrong. (*Victoria walks out.*)
WALLACE. Too *fast*? (*Pause.*) I mistook love for a girl who ate *Jujyfruits.* (*Wallace drinks from his bottle.*)

SCENE EIGHT

> *Grandmother's kitchen. Wallace is sitting at the table. Grandmother walks in with a glass of milk and a plate of cookies.*

GRANDMOTHER. Tollhouse cookies, baked this morning especially for *you.*
WALLACE. Thanks.
GRANDMOTHER. You look wonderful. Such a *handsome* thing.
WALLACE. This is delicious.
GRANDMOTHER. Of *course* it is. Would I serve you anything *but*? The first batch went to Grandpa, so *terrible*. (*Pause.*) I'm so *happy* you came to visit.
WALLACE. I love to visit you guys.
GRANDMOTHER. That's like sugar on my heart. It makes me feel so good. (*Wallace points to a photograph in a frame on the table.*)
WALLACE. Who's this?
GRANDMOTHER. That's Grandpa's second cousin, Jerry. He just died. That's the last picture of him, taken *two minutes* before he went. He was at a wedding there, sitting at his table, in between two pretty young girls — you see? The photographer snapped this picture, Jerry was joking and flirting with these young girls — he was like that, Jerry, so *bad* — two minutes later, he just *shut his eyes.* (*Pause.*) *Gone.* But still smiling.
WALLACE. (*Pause.*) Nice picture. (*Pause.*) Grandma, can I ask you something stupid?
GRANDMOTHER. If it makes you happy, I don't see why *not.*
WALLACE. What was your first kiss like?
GRANDMOTHER. My first *kiss*? You really have faith in my memory, don't you?

16

WALLACE. You don't have to tell me.

GRANDMOTHER. No, no, no. Let's see. It was with Grandpa, and we were —

WALLACE. Your first kiss was with *Grandpa*?

GRANDMOTHER. Sure. We were steadies in *high* school, you know.

WALLACE. I just never really thought about it. (*Pause.*) Was it nice?

GRANDMOTHER. I was petrified, but he made me feel comfortable. Still petrified, but in a comfortable way. Comfortably petrified. It was on a Saturday night, in nineteen-thirty-six, I think. We were in Wentworth Park, about four blocks from here.

WALLACE. Wow.

GRANDMOTHER. I remember thinking he kissed really wonderfully. I mean, we were just in high school, and kissing him made me feel like the movie stars must have felt. I almost fell *backwards*, I was so taken away. Then I got suspicious, asking myself where'd he *learn* to kiss like that. When I asked him —

WALLACE. You *asked* him?

GRANDMOTHER. I *asked* him, and he told me he had been practicing on his pillow for almost five years. That made me feel better. Besides, with those eyes, I couldn't help but believe him. (*Pause.*) I was sixteen then. Generations are different.

WALLACE. Yeah.

GRANDMOTHER. Each generation changes. It either improves or declines.

WALLACE. Yeah, trouble is, you can't tell one from the other. I mean, what *your* generation calls decline, *mine* calls improvement. It's so confusing. Along with everything else.

GRANDMOTHER. Don't waste your time thinking of it. I will say one thing, though. Hair is important. Secondary, but important nonetheless. Find a girl with *hair*.

WALLACE. *Hair*?

GRANDMOTHER. Sure. I mean, I can't run my fingers through Grandpa's hair. All I can do is rub his scalp. (*Pause.*) Which some say brings good luck.

WALLACE. I think that's when you rub *Buddha's* scalp.

GRANDMOTHER. Well, Grandpa's certainly not *Buddha*. And I'm certainly not *lucky*.

WALLACE. (*Pause.*) Do you ever miss Mommy?

GRANDMOTHER. All the time.

WALLACE. (*Pause.*) Me, too. (*Pause.*) All the time.

GRANDMOTHER. (*Pause.*) Drink your milk. It's good for your teeth.

SCENE NINE

Wallace.

WALLACE. "My Mother's Turtlenecks." By Wallace Kirkman. Age sixteen. My mother loved my father and hated her neck. She thought it was too fleshy or something. If I hated *my* neck, I'd have it removed, but my mother never trusted doctors, so she wore turtlenecks. All the time. In every picture we have of her, she's wearing a turtleneck. She had turtlenecks in every color of the rainbow, she had blacks, she had whites, she had greys, she had plaids, she had polka dots and hound's-tooth checks and stripes and Mickey Mouse and even a sort of *mesh* turtleneck. I can't picture her without a turtleneck on. Although, according to Freud, I *try* to, every moment of every day. We have a photograph of me when I was a baby wearing one of my mother's turtlenecks. *Swimming* in one of my mother's turtlenecks is more like it. Just a bald head and a big shirt. It's very erotic in an Oedipal shirtwear sort of way. It's a rare photograph, because I'm smiling. I didn't smile all that much during most of my childhood. I'm taking lessons now, trying to learn again, but it takes time. I stopped smiling when my mother stopped wearing turtlenecks. I came home from a typical day in the second grade to find her taking a bath in her own blood on the kitchen floor. Her turtleneck was on top of the kitchen table, so it wouldn't come between her neck and her knife. I understood then why she had worn turtlenecks all along. To stop the blood from flowing. To cover the wound that was there all along. They tried to cover the wound when they buried her with one of her favorite turtleneck dresses on, but

18

it didn't matter. It was just an empty hole by then. My mother wasn't hiding inside. (*Pause.*) She wrote a note before she died, asking to be cremated, and I asked my father why she wasn't. He said my mother was two women, and the one he loved would have been scared of the flames. (*Pause.*) I look at that photograph of little me inside my mother's shirt all the time. It's the closest I can get to security. There are no pictures of me inside mother's womb, but her turtleneck is close enough.

SCENE TEN

Wallace's bedroom. Wallace and Sarah are sitting on the bed. Sarah is reading something on a piece of paper.

SARAH. Oh, I *really* like it.
WALLACE. *Really?*
SARAH. *Really.* It's very good.
WALLACE. *Why?*
SARAH. Well, it's funny, but it's also *sad.* It's really *sad.* And it's so *true.* I mean, there's so much of *you* in there. I mean, if I didn't know you, I'd *know* you after I read this. You know what I mean? I think it's really talented work. What's it for?
WALLACE. *For?*
SARAH. I mean, is it for English class or something?
WALLACE. No. I just sort of *wrote* it. Not really *for* anything. For me, I guess.
SARAH. You should submit it to the school newspaper. I bet they'd publish it.
WALLACE. I don't think I want the whole school reading this.
SARAH. Why not? I mean, you shouldn't be *ashamed* or anything—
WALLACE. I'm not *ashamed.* It just seems a little *sensationalist,* you know?
SARAH. I don't know. I guess so.
WALLACE. *So.* (*Pause.*) What do you want to do?
SARAH. Oh, I don't know.
WALLACE. We could go see a movie.
SARAH. Sure.

19

WALLACE. Or we could stay here.

SARAH. Sure.

WALLACE. Well, which one?

SARAH. Whichever.

WALLACE. Come on, I'm horrible with decisions.

SARAH. So am I.

WALLACE. Sarah, you're the valedictorian of our *class*, for Chrissakes. If you can't make a decision, who can?

SARAH. Umm, do you want to . . . stay *here*?

WALLACE. Yes.

SARAH. Okay. Let's stay here, then.

WALLACE. Settled. Do you want something to drink?

SARAH. Umm, sure.

WALLACE. What do you want? Some wine? A screwdriver?

SARAH. Oh, you mean something to *drink*. I don't drink.

WALLACE. Oh. (*Pause.*) Do you mind if I drink something?

SARAH. Oh, no, don't let me stand in your way.

WALLACE. I'll be right back.

SARAH. Okay. (*Wallace walks out. Sarah looks around the room. She looks at a photograph in a frame by the bed. Wallace walks in, sipping a glass of wine.*)

WALLACE. *In vino veritas.*

SARAH. Who's this?

WALLACE. It's my mother.

SARAH. She was beautiful.

WALLACE. She was okay. I'm going to light a candle, okay?

SARAH. Sure. (*Wallace gets a candle. He takes a lighter from his pocket.*)

WALLACE. My great-grandfather was lighting a pipe with this lighter when he died. It's a Zippo. Pretty sharp, huh?

SARAH. It's very nice. (*Wallace tries to light the lighter. It won't light.*)

WALLACE. I think it has to warm up. (*Pause. Wallace tries to light the lighter a few more times. It won't light.*) Uhh, I guess my great-grandfather forgot to refill it before he died. It's just as well. I hate candles. They're so *cliched*. (*Pause.*) You want to listen to some music?

SARAH. Sure.

WALLACE. What do you like?

SARAH. Oh, *anything*.

WALLACE. You like James Taylor?

SARAH. Sure.

WALLACE. Let me just find the tape. (*Wallace looks for the tape.*) I don't know where I put it. Maybe it's out in the car. I can go check—

SARAH. That's okay. We don't *need* music. Do we?

WALLACE. Uhh, *no*, I guess *not*. (*Pause.*) Well.

SARAH. What was your mother like, Wallace?

WALLACE. What was she *like*?

SARAH. Yeah.

WALLACE. She was like Sylvia Plath without a Fulbright scholarship.

SARAH. What do you mean?

WALLACE. I mean—I don't know what I mean, I'm *sixteen*. (*Wallace drinks his glass of wine.*) Would you mind if I kissed you?

SARAH. The wine works fast.

WALLACE. No, *I* do. Can I?

SARAH. Umm, can't we *talk* for a while—

WALLACE. I don't *want* to talk, I want to *kiss*. Can I kiss you?

SARAH. I'd really feel better if we just—

WALLACE. Oh, come *on*— (*Wallace kisses Sarah, long and hard.*)

SARAH. Maybe I should go.

WALLACE. What? Oh, come on—

SARAH. No, I mean, maybe this wasn't such a good idea.

WALLACE. Don't you *like* me?

SARAH. Very much, Wallace. But I don't want this to be just—I don't know, a lot of *stupidity*. Just kissing and nothing else. I wanted to *talk* to you, you know?

WALLACE. Yeah, whatever.

SARAH. Oh, Wallace, don't do that—

WALLACE. Just go, please.

SARAH. What?

WALLACE. You said maybe you should leave, so leave. I don't want to—I just don't want to *deal* with this, okay?

SARAH. But—

WALLACE. But *nothing*. Just, please, go, okay?

SARAH. I—*fine*. Bye, Wallace.

WALLACE. Yeah, yeah, see you —
SARAH. I'm sorry this didn't work out. (*Pause.*) I'll see you
in school on Monday. Okay? (*Pause.*) Okay, bye. (*Sarah walks
out.*)

SCENE ELEVEN

*Wallace's bedroom. Wallace is sitting on his bed, talking
on the phone.*

WALLACE. Yeah, I wanted to see if I could make a song
request and a dedication . . . Umm, "Something In The
Way She Moves". . . . By James Taylor. . . . You *don't*?
I mean, it's on "Greatest Hits". You see, I'm trying to right a
wrong, as they say. . . . I don't know, it's an expres-
sion. . . . Umm, do you have any, I don't know, like, Cat
Stevens or something, somebody *close* to James Taylor? You
know, one man and a guitar, that sort of thing. . . . Only
top forty? . . . Who's in the top forty? Anybody named
James? . . . No, that's not really appropriate. . . . Umm,
could I just make a dedication, then? . . . Well, I *know* it's
supposed to be for a song, but you don't seem to have the
song I *need*, so if I could just maybe make the dedication and
then you could maybe not play anything for about three
minutes in *place* of the song I need and that way — *hello*?
(*Pause.*) *Shit.* (*Wallace hangs up the phone.*)

SCENE TWELVE

Sarah's front door. Sarah inside, Wallace outside.

SARAH. Wallace.
WALLACE. Sarah.
SARAH. What are you doing here?
WALLACE. I wanted — umm, I wanted to *apologize.*
SARAH. You don't *have* to —
WALLACE. Yeah, I do.
SARAH. Okay. (*Pause.*) So?
WALLACE. You know, I just — it's funny, you know, some-

times I just wish I were a little kid again, when "sorry" was okay, you know?

SARAH. Yeah, well, we're not little kids, Wallace.

WALLACE. We're *not*? Umm, no, no, we're *not*. We're *certainly* not. Umm — *okay. Well.* I was acting *really* stupid before, I mean, just very — *stupid*. It was — I was being, umm —

SARAH. Stupid.

WALLACE. *Yeah.* And it was *wrong*, and it was — you know, it made you — it was *unfair*. And I *apologize*.

SARAH. Okay —

WALLACE. And I thought maybe we could try *again*.

SARAH. Again?

WALLACE. Yeah, you know, maybe I could come *in* —

SARAH. My parents are sleeping.

WALLACE. Oh. (*Pause.*) I could try to be quiet.

SARAH. It's kind of *late*.

WALLACE. Umm, well, you know, maybe you could come back over to my house and we could start from the *beginning*.

SARAH. *Wallace* —

WALLACE. I mean, I know it *sounds* like a stupid idea, but trust me, I'll behave this time, I know what to do. We can *talk*. We can have a *conversation*. We don't even have to kiss, we'll just *talk* and then you can go. (*Pause.*) Or we can just sit in *silence* for a while. We don't *have* to talk.

SARAH. I don't think that's a very good *idea*, Wallace.

WALLACE. All I'm *asking* for is another chance, Sarah. Don't make me beg.

SARAH. There's no need to *beg*, Wallace, I just don't think —

WALLACE. Okay. I'll beg. (*Wallace drops to his knees.*) I'm *begging*, Sarah, give me another shot.

SARAH. Wallace —

WALLACE. I'll be *good*.

SARAH. *Wallace* —

WALLACE. Look at the moon, Sarah. It's *full*. It's *romantic*.

SARAH. Wallace, get off your knees.

WALLACE. (*Pause.*) That's okay. I kind of like it down here. (*Pause.*) I was going to bring a guitar and maybe *serenade* you, but I can't sing. And I don't play the guitar. I did have Romantic Thoughts, though.

SARAH. That's very sweet, Wallace. (*Pause.*) I really should go back *inside*—

WALLACE. Yeah, I understand. You know, I tried to dedicate a song to you on the radio, you know, something by James Taylor, and they didn't *have* any James Taylor. Can you *believe* that?

SARAH. That's pretty funny.

WALLACE. Yeah. Pretty Funny World.

SARAH. Sure is.

WALLACE. So, umm, you wouldn't want to maybe try again, say, *next* weekend? A movie or—

SARAH. *Wallace.*

WALLACE. No, I understand. Okay.

SARAH. I'm *sorry*, Wallace.

WALLACE. Yeah, no, *I'm* sorry.

SARAH. (*Pause.*) Are you going to *stay* down there?

WALLACE. For a little while, yeah. If you don't mind.

SARAH. No, I don't mind.

WALLACE. Thanks.

SARAH. Yeah, well, okay. Goodnight, Wallace.

WALLACE. 'Night.

SARAH. Bye.

WALLACE. Bye. (*Sarah walks out, closing the door behind her. Pause. Wallace looks up at the moon.*) Thanks a lot, Moon. You really came through for me.

SCENE THIRTEEN

Psychiatrist's office. Psychiatrist is sitting in a chair, writing in a notebook. Wallace walks in.

PSYCHIATRIST. Hello, Wallace. It's been a long time since I've seen you.

WALLACE. About five years.

PSYCHIATRIST. Yes. Nice to see you again.

WALLACE. I'll bet.

PSYCHIATRIST. Would you like to have a seat?

WALLACE. No.

PSYCHIATRIST. Okay, then. What's on your mind?

WALLACE. Lots. (*Pause.*) I came here last time because my father made me, but now I'm here because I want to talk to you. You see, I'm confused. My mother makes me a sandwich for lunch. I take it. She, in turn, slits her throat. And after the funeral, when I go back to school for the first time, my *father* makes me a sandwich for lunch, or at least he *tries*, so as not to screw up my daily routine any more than it already has been. And I'm thinking, all day while I'm in school, that *he's* going to be lying on the kitchen floor when I get home. It's the same thing, you see, because I *took* the sandwich. If I didn't *take*, I think, they'll be okay. But I *take*, and that kills them. And when I came home from school and he *wasn't* on the floor of the kitchen, but instead sitting in his study, *alive*, I was disappointed. Let down. Because my system didn't work. It *failed* me. Everything was *failing* me. And when I *expected* my father to fail me, he failed me by *not* failing me. He was just sitting there in his study. Alone, deserted by the woman he loved and planned to — I don't know, move to Florida with, and he can manage to stay alive, to go on living. *How?* And, I mean, Victoria, this twelve year old *girl*, is *sitting* there, practically *begging* me to kiss her, I mean, she would have been on her *knees* in a second, in more ways than one, that's how it seemed, and when I finally let down and actually *do* what she's been *asking* me to do — I *kiss* her and *bang* — all of a sudden, *I'm* too goddamn *fast* for her. I told her I *loved* her, and she runs off, *skipping*, and the next week she's kissing somebody else, and I heard he got up her *shirt*, and *he's* not too fast, *I'm* the one who was too *fast*. So I get this reputation that scares the hell out of me, because, not only will no *decent* girls *look* at me, I can't even think about any of the *in*decent girls, because I'm scared to death of having to live up to my own reputation. And, now, I mean, when my big mistake has always been talking too much, so I try, finally, on this girl I *really* like, okay, I mean, *bright, pretty*, actually *nice, caring*, I try not to screw it up by talking too much, and I go *right* for the kiss and she won't ever see me again because I didn't talk too much. I mean, I can't *win*. They *desert*. Women *desert*. And I know it all stems back to my fucking *coward* mother, and if she hadn't *offed* herself, I'd

25

have no problems, but what I'm trying to say is I don't know what the hell to *do* about all of this, Doctor, and it's my life, so can — you know, can you give me some *advice* or something, Doctor? (*Pause.*) Doctor? (*Pause.*) Doctor?

SCENE FOURTEEN

Wallace and Psychiatrist.

WALLACE. "Tyrannosaurus Rex." By Wallace Kirkman. Age eighteen. (*Psychiatrist gets up and starts to walk out.*) Don't go. I need *help* with this one. Stay right there. Please. You'll like this. It's very *Freudian*. In fact, it's a *dream*. (*The lights change rather dramatically. Psychiatrist sits and Wallace walks out. He walks in a moment later with a crate of props.*) I need a *mother*. (*Pause.*) I need somebody who can *act* like a mother. *Please*. (*Victoria walks in.*) You'll do. I always wanted to be a dinosaur when I was young. You*nger*. I have a lot in common with Tyrannosaurus. We both walk on two legs, we both eat meat, and we both occasionally answer to the nickname "King of the Tyrant Lizards." Anyhow, the recipe for this dream is something like two parts "Oedipus Rex," two parts Freud, and nineteen parts me. In the beginning, the eventual parents are both thirteen years old. (*Wallace pushes Psychiatrist and Victoria onto their knees.*) And Jewish. (*Wallace pulls two pairs of gag glasses out of the crate of props. He puts one—with a plastic nose—on Victoria and the other—with a plastic nose and a plastic moustache—on Psychiatrist.*) They get bar mitzvahed and bat mitzvahed on the same day and sleep with each other on the same night. Kids today. God bless 'em. On with the dream. The girl gets pregnant, as girls will do. (*Wallace pulls a baby doll out of the crate of props and hands it to Victoria.*) She wants to get an abortion so the baby won't get in the way of the seventh grade, but neither of the partners got any cash for their *mitzvahs*, only savings bonds. *Lots* of savings bonds. So, they pack several pairs of underwear and go to stay with the girl's grandmother, a mentally ill fortune teller from Boston. (*Grandmother walks in — a grand entrance —wearing a turban.*)

26

GRANDMOTHER. This baby is *trouble*. He's going to fight with you and *shtoop* you.

VICTORIA. *Shtoop?*

PSYCHIATRIST. How do you know the baby's going to be a "he"?

GRANDMOTHER. I'm a fortune teller. Give me a break.

WALLACE. When the baby is born, they immediately sell it on the black market. (*Victoria tosses the baby doll to Wallace. Wallace pulls a packet of play money out of the crate of props and hands it to Victoria.*) They use the money to pay a few months worth of rent on a Beacon Street apartment. (*Wallace takes the packet of play money from Victoria and replaces it in the crate of props. He pulls a pair of boxing gloves out of the crate of props and hands them to Psychiatrist, who puts them on.*) The father starts to take boxing lessons. The mother spends her spare time in their spare apartment reading spare Japanese literature. (*Wallace pulls a Mishima paperback out of the crate of props and tosses it to Victoria.*) They earn rent money and grocery money and boxing lesson money and Japanese book money by becoming kiddie porn stars. (*Psychiatrist and Victoria look at one another in* horror.) *Cut.* And, at this point, the dream leaps ahead about seventeen years or so. The father is a very popular amateur boxer. (*Wallace pulls Psychiatrist up off her knees so she is standing. Wallace pulls Victoria up off her knees so she is also standing.*) The mother is about to commit ritual suicide. (*Wallace pulls the large knife Mother used to slit her throat out of the crate of props and hands it to Victoria.*)

VICTORIA. I've tried and tried and *tried*. And I'll just *never* be Japanese. (*Victoria plunges the large knife into her bowels and falls to the floor. Dead. Wallace stares at her for a moment, then tosses the baby doll into the crate of props and pulls out a pair of boxing gloves. He puts them on.*)

WALLACE. The son is a boxing necrophiliac who masturbates. A lot. (*Wallace approaches Grandmother.*) Hello.

GRANDMOTHER. *Shalom.*

WALLACE. (*To the audience.*) I *hate* when people say "shalom". I never know whether they're *coming* or *going* or just a *pacifist*.

GRANDMOTHER. How may I serve you?

WALLACE. I'd like to know my fortune.

GRANDMOTHER. Easy. You're going to fight with your Dad and *shtoop* your Mom. Ten bucks, please.

WALLACE. This is *horrible.* I don't want to fight with Dad. I *love* Dad.

GRANDMOTHER. Ten bucks, please.

WALLACE. And I don't want to *shtoop* Mom. Because Dad would get mad. And we'd fight.

GRANDMOTHER. Ten bucks, please.

WALLACE. And I don't want to fight with Dad. I *love* Dad. Boy, this makes me tense. I need some *release.*

GRANDMOTHER. Ten bucks, please. (*Wallace punches Grandmother and knocks her out.*)

WALLACE. I wonder if there's anything good over at the morgue. (*Wallace looks at Victoria.*) She's *beautiful.* She's *everything.* She's *dead. And* she's a nice Jewish girl. I wonder where her bowels are. (*Wallace leaps onto Victoria, kisses her madly for a few moments, then rolls off onto the floor.*) It's time to *box.* (*Wallace approaches Psychiatrist. A bell rings. Psychiatrist punches Wallace and knocks him out.*)

PSYCHIATRIST. 10, 9, 8, 7, 6, 5, 4, 3, 2, 1. (*Psychiatrist slaps Wallace's face and he comes to.*)

WALLACE. Did I win?

PSYCHIATRIST. Nope.

WALLACE. *Shit.*

PSYCHIATRIST. Come on, I'll buy you a beer.

WALLACE. I'm underage.

PSYCHIATRIST. You don't have a fake i.d.?

WALLACE. I was always too busy *masturbating* to buy one.

PSYCHIATRIST. Oh. (*Pause.*) Come on, I'll buy you a ginger ale.

WALLACE. Yeah, okay. You're on. (*Psychiatrist helps Wallace up and they walk a few steps.*)

PSYCHIATRIST. One beer and one ginger ale, barkeep.

WALLACE. Excuse me for a moment, I've got to go to the bathroom.

PSYCHIATRIST. But you haven't had anything to drink.

WALLACE. (*Pause.*) *Excuse me for a moment, I've got to go to the bathroom.*

PSYCHIATRIST. Oh. Sure, go right ahead.

WALLACE. Be right back. (*Wallace walks out. He runs in a few moments later, without the boxing gloves on, his hands covering his eyes. He is screaming. Grandmother, Psychiatrist, and Victoria clear the stage and walk out. The lights change back. Wallace takes his hands off his tightly closed eyes, opens them, sees nobody around, and stops screaming. He yawns, as if waking up.*) I've been having this dream every night for the past two months. It's always pretty much the same, although sometimes it's in color and sometimes it's in black-and-white, and once the black-and-white version was colorized, which pissed me off. I mean, it's more or less my life story, and who wants their life story *colorized*?

SCENE FIFTEEN

Wallace's dormitory room. Wallace and Lili walk in.

WALLACE. This is my room.
LILI. Nice. How did you get a single room your first year?
WALLACE. I had a psychiatrist write the school a note saying essentially that if I had to live with another person I'd probably kill them.
LILI. Seriously?
WALLACE. Not really. But the school believed it. (*Pause.*) You must be tired.
LILI. Why?
WALLACE. Well, I mean, you were on the stage for practically the entire time.
LILI. It's an important part.
WALLACE. And you did it so well. *Really.* The whole thing was — *beautiful.*
LILI. The choreographer's pretty talented.
WALLACE. I mean, who the hell would ever think to do "Catcher in the Rye" as a *ballet*?
LILI. The *choreographer* would.
WALLACE. I — well, I mean, I *know*, but it's just — *wow.* You know, I never realized there was so much stuff about *lesbians* in "Catcher in the Rye."
LILI. It's all in the *subtext.*
WALLACE. Yeah. But I think, you know, having *you* — you

29

know, having a *woman* as Holden Caulfield really made everything *quite* clear.

LILI. I'm glad you liked it. (*Pause.*) You're very *cute*, Wallace.

WALLACE. *Me?*

LILI. Yes, you. I'm really *drawn* to you, you know?

WALLACE. Umm, *sure.*

LILI. What are you waiting for?

WALLACE. Huh?

LILI. *Kiss* me.

WALLACE. Umm, are you — umm, *sure.* (*Wallace kisses Lili.*) How was that?

LILI. That was nice. Do you want to sleep together?

WALLACE. *What?*

LILI. Do you want to *make love?*

WALLACE. Umm, with *you?*

LILI. *Yes*, with *me.*

WALLACE. Umm, sure, yes, yeah, *sure.* (*Pause.*) What do we do?

LILI. Are you a *virgin?*

WALLACE. Umm, *technically*, no.

LILI. What do you mean, "technically?"

WALLACE. Well, what is the definition of male virginity?

LILI. Is that a rhetorical question?

WALLACE. A male virgin is a male who has never had his thing inside a female's thing. Right?

LILI. Anybody still calling it a "thing" is probably a virgin, I know that much.

WALLACE. Well, when I was born, I had a thing. A very tiny, bald thing, but a thing nonetheless. And I entered this world through my mother's thing — the infamous "tunnel of love". Therefore, my thing has been inside of a female's thing, although it had to share the space with the rest of my body. In fact, pretty much all men are born nonvirgins. The only exceptions would be men born Caesarean style.

LILI. You're saying you lost your virginity — with your *mother?*

WALLACE. Yeah.

LILI. You're pretty weird, Wallace.

WALLACE. Thank you.

LILI. So, will this be your first time having sex with some-body outside your immediate family?

WALLACE. You've got me there. Yes.

LILI. I'm *honored.*

WALLACE. I'm *terrified.*

LILI. It's simple. Don't worry, you'll be fine. Before we get started, do you have any protection?

WALLACE. Umm, no.

LILI. Here, take this. (*Lili hands Wallace a condom.*)

WALLACE. You really come prepared.

LILI. I don't want to even joke *around* with AIDS, you know?

WALLACE. I know. Remember when AYDS was just a di-etetic candy? There's a stock that must have done *real* well. Can you picture the president of the company right before the end? "Call the damn thing Dexatrim, it's a *superb* name for a disease!"

LILI. You don't have to make jokes, Wallace, everything's going to be fine. *Better* than fine.

WALLACE. How did you know I was nervous? I thought I was covering it pretty well.

LILI. A woman knows.

WALLACE. Hey, tell me something.

LILI. Yeah?

WALLACE. What can you possibly see in me?

LILI. What do you mean?

WALLACE. I mean, how did I end up here with *you?* You're a beautiful senior, I'm a nervous little freshman.

LILI. You've got great eyes.

WALLACE. I *do?*

LILI. Really intelligent eyes. Like they've seen a *lot,* that's what they look like.

WALLACE. You're here with me because of my *eyes?*

LILI. Yeah, sort of.

WALLACE. The brochures don't do college justice.

LILI. Let's get on the *bed,* Wallace.

WALLACE. Let me just hit the lights.

LILI. No, keep them *on,* I want to *see* you.

WALLACE. You keep the lights on with a guy named Biff who pumps iron and gasoline. With a Jew from Jersey, you

31

do it in the dark. (*Wallace flips the light switch. Blackout.*)

LILI. (*Pause.*) Why do you wear so many *layers?*

WALLACE. Wearing layers of clothing keeps you warmer than wearing one *thick* garment.

LILI. But it's not cold out.

WALLACE. Alright, so I hate my body. I'm too skinny. Is that such a crime?

LILI. You've got a nice body.

WALLACE. In the *dark*, maybe. You're so *sweaty—*

LILI. I want to *see* you, Wallace, I want to see *all* of you. Can't you turn the lights on?

WALLACE. If the lights go on, I go in the closet.

LILI. Do you have a candle or something, at least?

WALLACE. I *hate* candles. (*Pause.*) Am I doing okay?

LILI. You're doing *fine*. Just *fine*.

WALLACE. (*Pause.*) Why did the chicken cross the road?

LILI. This isn't the *time*, Wallace.

WALLACE. Sorry. (*Long pause. Wallace flips the light switch. The lights come up. They sit up in bed together.*) Wow. (*Pause.*) You know, I always wondered what this would be like, I always tried to imagine, and it's just—now it's *actual*. Now it's *real*. Now—I just slept with an older woman. An older woman who *dances*. Billy Corkscraw would never believe it.

LILI. *Who?*

WALLACE. This kid I was friends with growing up, Billy Corkscraw. He talked about sex all the time. He told me everything, little Mister Know-It-All. You know, told me that the only way to *really* satisfy a woman was to put Spanish Fly in her drink, and if you were dating a girl who spoke French instead of Spanish, you had to get your Spanish Fly "translated" which Billy said could only be done at the French embassy and it cost a hell of a lot of money, and he said we would probably just be better off paying professionals. (*Pause.*) He moved to Arizona when we were eleven. Last I heard about him, he couldn't find a date for his senior prom.

LILI. (*Pause.*) You have to meet my little *sister*.

Wallace's dormitory room. Wallace and Nina are sitting on the bed. She is looking at a photograph in a frame by the bed.

NINA. Is this your mother?
WALLACE. Yeah. She's dead.
NINA. Oh. I'm sorry.
WALLACE. For what?
NINA. For asking.
WALLACE. I don't mind. I mean, I've lived without her for so long — it's not all that bad, really.
NINA. What was she like?
WALLACE. Like Sylvia Plath without talent.
NINA. She killed herself?
WALLACE. Yeah. When I was six.
NINA. That's too bad. How'd she kill herself?
WALLACE. You really want to know?
NINA. Yeah. If you don't want to talk about it, though —
WALLACE. No, I do. It's just that it freaks most people out. (*Pause.*) She slit her throat with a kitchen knife.
NINA. Oh, God. I never understand why people don't just take pills and die painlessly.
WALLACE. I guess if you hate yourself enough to want to die — it's just like if you wanted to kill someone else. If you hate something, you want it to die painfully. I mean, I guess that's what it is. I know that pain belongs in there somewhere.
NINA. How did you deal with all that? I mean, how'd you get through it?
WALLACE. I used to break glass.
NINA. Huh?
WALLACE. I used to break glasses on the kitchen floor. That helped a little. It was destructive, but it eased the pain.
NINA. How *sad* —
WALLACE. It's no big deal. I mean, I guess it made me who I am today, and who knows what I would have been if she was still alive. Maybe I'd be somebody I'd hate, you know. Sure,

there are times I'd kill to have her back, just for a day. So I could show her something I've written, or talk to her about my thoughts, or just even to see her smile when I did something silly. (*Long pause.*)

NINA. What are you thinking about?

WALLACE. I don't know. About my mother, and about how you listen to me talk, and—and about how I'd love to kiss you right now.

NINA. So why *don't* you?

WALLACE. What? Well, umm, Nina, do you—did your sister tell you—

NINA. I know. You and my sister were—*together.*

WALLACE. And it doesn't *bother* you?

NINA. A little. Not much. I mean, you were drunk—

WALLACE. *What?*

NINA. And all you did was *kiss*, right?

WALLACE. Umm—umm, *yeah.* Just a few drunken kisses, that's all it was.

NINA. A *few?* She said *one.*

WALLACE. Well, I mean, there were a few *within* the one. But we never pulled our lips apart, so technically, I guess, yeah, just *one.*

NINA. Okay. (*Pause.*) Well?

WALLACE. Well what?

NINA. *Kiss* me.

WALLACE. Nina, I think I *love* you. I know it sounds stupid, but—is that okay?

NINA. Sure.

WALLACE. Okay. I'm going to kiss you now, okay?

NINA. Okay.

WALLACE. Okay. (*They kiss.*)

Scene Seventeen

Wallace's dormitory room. Wallace and Wendy are sitting on the bed, kissing.

WENDY. Are you sure we should be doing this?

WALLACE. Why not?

WENDY. Well, what about your girlfriend?

WALLACE. What *about* her?
WENDY. Well—
WALLACE. I'm drunk, you're drunk, we don't know what we're doing. Right?
WENDY. Umm, *right.*
WALLACE. *Right.* Give me a kiss. (*They kiss.*)

SCENE EIGHTEEN

Wallace in a spotlight.

WALLACE. I fucked up. Mommy. I fell in love—*really*—for the first time. I mean, it wasn't romance for the sake of romance. It was romance for the sake of—*somebody. Nina.* Nina listened. And I got scared. I ran away. To somebody else. What do I do? Mommy. It *hurts.* (*Pause.*) I want my—I *need* my mother. (*Pause.*) I'm not asking for much. I just—all I want is to take the knife away from her. To go back and take the knife away from her. All I want to do is change history. (*The lights come up on the kitchen. Mother is fixing a peanut butter and banana sandwich. She is peeling the banana. Wallace looks at her. He looks at the audience, then looks back at her. He walks past the table picking up the large knife as he goes by. He walks out. Mother finishes peeling the banana and fixes the sandwich, breaking the banana up with her hands and spreading the peanut butter with a spoon. She puts the sandwich into a lunchbox on the table. Wallace runs in.*) I'm going to miss the bus! Is my lunch ready?
MOTHER. All set. (*Wallace grabs the lunchbox and kisses Mother on the cheek.*)
WALLACE. Bye, Mommy.
MOTHER. Bye, Wallace.
WALLACE. (*To the audience.*) I love the second grade!
MOTHER. Don't shout, Wallace. (*Wallace runs out. Mother watches after him. She writes a note on a slip of paper. While she is writing the note, Wallace walks in and quietly watches her from the side. She puts the note on the table. She takes off her turtleneck shirt, so she is in her brassiere. She wraps the turtleneck around her neck and pulls it taut, attempting to strangle herself. The lights on the kitchen slowly fade, and Wallace is in the spotlight again.*)
WALLACE. (*To the audience. Pause.*) In countless science

35

fiction stories about time travel, the moral is quite clear. When you go back in time, if you so much as step on an ant, the course of history will change drastically. Don't try to change history. It's dangerous. (*Pause.*) In my experience, trying to change history isn't really dangerous. It's just a waste of time — a futile, frustrating exercise where you exert yourself and use up boundless energies and — and everything stays exactly the same. With small technical differences, perhaps. One more dead ant. If you take a razor away from a man who wants to kill himself, he'll *still* kill himself — he just won't be clean shaven. The will is all that matters. If the will is there — (*Pause.*) I should dwell on the future. Dwelling on the past is hopeless.

SCENE NINETEEN

Wallace's dormitory room. Wallace is standing. There is a knock on the door.

WALLACE. Yeah. (*Nina walks in.*)
NINA. Hey, there.
WALLACE. Sit down.
NINA. What's wrong?
WALLACE. Sit down.
NINA. Okay. (*Nina sits on the bed.*) What's the matter?
WALLACE. You deserve better.
NINA. Huh?
WALLACE. I'm not good enough for you.
NINA. What are you talking about? You're the *best.*
WALLACE. I'm the *worst.* You should *hate* me.
NINA. Why?
WALLACE. You don't want to know.
NINA. *What* don't I want to know?
WALLACE. I've been with somebody else.
NINA. (*Pause.*) What?
WALLACE. I was with somebody else.
NINA. (*Pause.*) Who?
WALLACE. Wendy.
NINA. Wendy. (*Pause.*) I think I'm going to be sick. (*Nina runs out.*)
WALLACE. *Nina.* (*Pause.*) Women *desert.* (*Wallace picks up a*

glass. *He holds it in his hand, looking at it. He starts to throw it so it will break against the wall. Nina walks in.*)

NINA. Don't you dare break that glass or I'll turn right around and I won't come back. (*Wallace stops. He puts the glass on the bed and looks at Nina.*)

WALLACE. You came back. (*Pause.*) You should hate me.

NINA. I do. But I also happen to love you, and I'm not going to lose you without a fight.

WALLACE. You came back.

NINA. Do you want to work through this? I'll tell you right now, it's not going to be easy.

WALLACE. I know.

NINA. You betrayed me.

WALLACE. I know.

NINA. I know you may have been scared or whatever, but I swear to God, if you ever do this again, both you and her — *whoever* she is — will be lying on the street, okay?

WALLACE. Okay. (*Pause.*) You came back.

NINA. You want to work through this?

WALLACE. Yes.

NINA. Okay. Then we will.

WALLACE. You came back. (*Wallace goes to hug Nina. They hug. After a few moments, she breaks from the hug and slaps him, hard, across the face.*)

NINA. Don't you *ever* do that to me again, understand?

WALLACE. You came back.

Scene Twenty

Grandmother's kitchen. Wallace and Grandmother are sitting at the table.

GRANDMOTHER. And you *really* love her?

WALLACE. I *swear*. At least, I think I do. I mean, I know I do. And I was running away from her. You know, I was so terrified that she'd leave me, I wanted to leave first so I wouldn't have to deal with the pain. You know, I *wanted* to get caught with this other girl, Grandma, I *had* to tell her about it right away. It all made sense when I told her. Too much sense. She said she was going to be sick and walked out of my room. And something in me clicked. Something in me

37

had been expecting it. Had been expecting her to leave me. And it made sense. And it was complete. (*Pause.*) And then she came *back.* That's what threw me for a loop. And right then I said, there is no way I am going to lose her. I am going to do everything in my power to keep her. Because she came *back.* And it scares the hell out of me that I almost lost her because Mommy killed herself. I mean, my mother deserts me for whatever reasons, but she almost made me lose the one girl I've ever really *loved.*

GRANDMOTHER. (*Pause.*) You can't *blame* her until you die, you know.

WALLACE. What?

GRANDMOTHER. Your mother. I mean, sure, you can invoke her name once in a while to clear up a messy situation, but you've got to be responsible for *something* eventually. A dead mother does not give you *carte blanche* for a lifetime of screwing up. You can *do* it — you can screw *up*, go right ahead, but don't keep blaming her, or you'll just go through life fooling yourself and you'll die a blind man. (*Pause.*) Understand?

WALLACE. I think so. I'm not sure.

GRANDMOTHER. It's okay. You're still young. (*Pause.*) Are they feeding you enough up at school? You look thin.

WALLACE. They're feeding me fine, Grandma. (*Pause. Wallace points to a photograph in a frame on the table.*) Who's this?

GRANDMOTHER. Oh, that's Gertrude Mawsbaum, we grew up together. She just passed on. This picture was taken three weeks before she died.

EPILOGUE

Wallace is standing to the left with a tomato in his hand and a crate of tomatoes at his feet. Nina is standing to the right, wearing a white dress. Pause.

NINA. Well?

WALLACE. (*Pause.*) I don't want to ruin your dress. (*Pause.*) I don't want to ruin your beautiful dress. (*Pause. The lights slowly fade.*)

38

PROPERTY PLOT

Prologue: Tomato (for Wallace to throw)
                Crate of tomatoes

Scene 2:   Kitchen table
                Large kitchen knife
                Peanut butter
                Banana
                Wonder bread
                Lunchbox

Scene 3:   Wallace's bed
                Gift-wrapped box of peanut brittle
                Photograph of Mommy

Scene 4:   School-yard bench
                Peanut butter/banana sandwich

Scene 6:   2 chairs
                Psychiatrist couch
                Notebook & pen

Scene 7:   Park bench
                Mallow cups
                Jujyfruits
                Bottle of pink drink

Scene 8:   Kitchen table & chairs
                Glass of milk
                Plate of Toll House cookies
                Framed photo of cousin Jerry

Scene 10:   Wallace's bed
                Bedside table
                Paper of Wallace's writing
                Framed photo of Mommy
                Telephone
                Candle
                Old Zippo lighter
                Telephone
                Glass of wine (set off-stage)

Scene 11:   (Same as Scene 10)

Scene 12:	Door unit
Scene 13:	(Same as Scene 6)

Scene 14:	(Same as Scene 13,) plus:
	Crate of props with:
	    1 pair gag glasses with nose
	    1 pair gag glasses with nose and mustache
	    Baby doll
	    Packet of play money
	    2 pair boxing gloves
	    Mishima paperback
	    Large kitchen knife (from Scene 2)

Scene 15:	Dorm bed Bedside table Bedside lamp Framed photo of Mommy Condom
Scene 16:	(Same as Scene 15)
Scene 18:	(Same as Scene 2)
Scene 19:	(Same as Scene 15,) plus: Drinking glass
Scene 20:	Kitchen table & chairs Framed photo of Gertrude Mawsbaum
Epilogue:	(Same as Prologue)

NEW PLAYS

★ **MATCH by Stephen Belber.** Mike and Lisa Davis interview a dancer and choreographer about his life, but it is soon evident that their agenda will either ruin or inspire them—and definitely change their lives forever. "Prolific laughs and ear-to-ear smiles." *–NY Magazine.* "Uproariously funny, deeply moving, enthralling theater. Stephen Belber's MATCH has great beauty and tenderness, and abounds in wit." *–NY Daily News.* "Three and a half out of four stars." *–USA Today.* "A theatrical steeplechase that leads straight from outrageous bitchery to unadorned, heartfelt emotion." *–Wall Street Journal.* [2M, 1W] ISBN: 0-8222-2020-2

★ **HANK WILLIAMS: LOST HIGHWAY by Randal Myler and Mark Harelik.** The story of the beloved and volatile country-music legend Hank Williams, featuring twenty-five of his most unforgettable songs. "[LOST HIGHWAY has] the exhilarating feeling of Williams on stage in a particular place on a particular night...serves up classic country with the edges raw and the energy hot...By the end of the play, you've traveled on a profound emotional journey: LOST HIGHWAY transports its audience and communicates the inspiring message of the beauty and richness of Williams' songs...forceful, clear-eyed, moving, impressive." *–Rolling Stone.* "...honors a very particular musical talent with care and energy... smart, sweet, poignant." *–NY Times.* [7M, 3W] ISBN: 0-8222-1985-9

★ **THE STORY by Tracey Scott Wilson.** An ambitious black newspaper reporter goes against her editor to investigate a murder and finds the *best* story...but at what cost? "A singular new voice...deeply emotional, deeply intellectual, and deeply musical..." *–The New Yorker.* "...a conscientious and absorbing new drama..." *–NY Times.* "...a riveting, tough-minded drama about race, reporting and the truth..." *–A.P.* "... a stylish, attention-holding script that ends on a chilling note that will leave viewers with much to talk about." *–Curtain Up.* [2M, 7W (doubling, flexible casting)] ISBN: 0-8222-1998-0

★ **OUR LADY OF 121st STREET by Stephen Adly Guirgis.** The body of Sister Rose, beloved Harlem nun, has been stolen, reuniting a group of life-challenged childhood friends who square off as they wait for her return. "A scorching and dark new comedy... Mr. Guirgis has one of the finest imaginations for dialogue to come along in years." *–NY Times.* "Stephen Guirgis may be the best playwright in America under forty." *–NY Magazine.* [8M, 4W] ISBN: 0-8222-1965-4

★ **HOLLYWOOD ARMS by Carrie Hamilton and Carol Burnett.** The coming-of-age story of a dreamer who manages to escape her bleak life and follow her romantic ambitions to stardom. Based on Carol Burnett's bestselling autobiography, *One More Time.* "...pure theatre and pure entertainment..." *–Talkin' Broadway.* "...a warm, fuzzy evening of theatre." *–BrodwayBeat.com.* "...chuckles and smiles of recognition or surprise flow naturally...a remarkable slice of life." *–TheatreScene.net.* [5M, 5W, 1 girl] ISBN: 0-8222-1959-X

★ **INVENTING VAN GOGH by Steven Dietz.** A haunting and hallucinatory drama about the making of art, the obsession to create and the fine line that separates truth from myth. "Like a van Gogh painting, Dietz's story is a gorgeous example of excess—one that remakes reality with broad, well-chosen brush strokes. At evening's end, we're left with the author's resounding opinions on art and artifice, and provoked by his constant query into which is greater: van Gogh's art or his violent myth." *–Phoenix New Times.* "Dietz's writing is never simple. It is always brilliant. Shaded, compressed, direct, lucid—he frames his subject with a remarkable understanding of painting as a physical experience." *–Tucson Citizen.* [4M, 1W] ISBN: 0-8222-1954-9

DRAMATISTS PLAY SERVICE, INC.
440 Park Avenue South, New York, NY 10016 212-683-8960 Fax 212-213-1539
postmaster@dramatists.com www.dramatists.com

NEW PLAYS

★ **AFTER ASHLEY by Gina Gionfriddo.** A teenager is unwillingly thrust into the national spotlight when a family tragedy becomes talk-show fodder. "A work that virtually any audience would find accessible." *–NY Times.* "Deft characterization and caustic humor." *–NY Sun.* "A smart satirical drama." *–Variety.* [4M, 2W] ISBN: 978-0-8222-2099-2

★ **THE RUBY SUNRISE by Rinne Groff.** Twenty-five years after Ruby struggles to realize her dream of inventing the first television, her daughter faces similar battles of faith as she works to get Ruby's story told on network TV. "Measured and intelligent, optimistic yet clear-eyed." *–NY Magazine.* "Maintains an exciting sense of ingenuity." *–Village Voice.* "Sinuous theatrical flair." *–Broadway.com.* [3M, 4W] ISBN: 978-0-8222-2140-1

★ **MY NAME IS RACHEL CORRIE taken from the writings of Rachel Corrie, edited by Alan Rickman and Katharine Viner.** This solo piece tells the story of Rachel Corrie who was killed in Gaza by an Israeli bulldozer set to demolish a Palestinian home. "Heartbreaking urgency. An invigoratingly detailed portrait of a passionate idealist." *–NY Times.* "Deeply authentically human." *–USA Today.* "A stunning dramatization." *–CurtainUp.* [1W] ISBN: 978-0-8222-2222-4

★ **ALMOST, MAINE by John Cariani.** This charming midwinter night's dream of a play turns romantic clichés on their ear as it chronicles the painfully hilarious amorous adventures (and misadventures) of residents of a remote northern town that doesn't quite exist. "A whimsical approach to the joys and perils of romance." *–NY Times.* "Sweet, poignant and witty." *–NY Daily News.* "Aims for the heart by way of the funny bone." *–Star-Ledger.* [2M, 2W] ISBN: 978-0-8222-2156-2

★ **Mitch Albom's TUESDAYS WITH MORRIE by Jeffrey Hatcher and Mitch Albom, based on the book by Mitch Albom.** The true story of Brandeis University professor Morrie Schwartz and his relationship with his student Mitch Albom. "A touching, life-affirming, deeply emotional drama." *–NY Daily News.* "You'll laugh. You'll cry." *–Variety.* "Moving and powerful." *–NY Post.* [2M] ISBN: 978-0-8222-2188-3

★ **DOG SEES GOD: CONFESSIONS OF A TEENAGE BLOCKHEAD by Bert V. Royal.** An abused pianist and a pyromaniac ex-girlfriend contribute to the teen-angst of America's most hapless kid. "A welcome antidote to the notion that the *Peanuts* gang provides merely American cuteness." *–NY Times.* "Hysterically funny." *–NY Post.* "The *Peanuts* kids have finally come out of their shells." *–Time Out.* [4M, 4W] ISBN: 978-0-8222-2152-4

DRAMATISTS PLAY SERVICE, INC.
440 Park Avenue South, New York, NY 10016 212-683-8960 Fax 212-213-1539
postmaster@dramatists.com www.dramatists.com